SUCCESSFUL HABITS FOR WORK

How 12 Practical Habits Can
Improve Your Productivity at Work

Darren Coddel

© Copyright 2021 - All rights reserved.

It is not legal to reproduce, duplicate, or transmit any part of this document in either electronic means or in printed format. Recording of this publication is strictly prohibited and any storage of this document is not allowed unless with written permission from the publisher except for the use of brief quotations in a book review.

Table of Contents

Introduction 1

Chapter One - The Habit of Anticipating Needs 3

Chapter Two - The Habit of Always Knowing the Answers 7

Chapter Three - The Habit of Reading the Room 13

Chapter Four - The Habit of Being Tidy 19

Chapter Five - The Habit of Befriending the Underlings 25

Chapter Six - The Habit of Self-Care 29

Chapter Seven - The Habit of Understanding Your Environment .. 35

Chapter Eight - The Habit of a Good Night's Sleep 39

Chapter Nine - The Habit of Understanding People's Habits 43

Chapter Ten - The Habit of Taking Criticism Well 49

Chapter Eleven - The Habit of Being Adaptable 53

Chapter Twelve - The Habit of Prioritizing 57

Final Words 61

About the Author 63

References 65

Introduction

> "We become what we repeatedly do."
> -Stephen Covey

IN THE WORKING WORLD, are you thriving or surviving? Whether you work in retail or a fast-paced office, we've all had times when we've wanted to throw in the towel, like when you're new at a company and you're trying to find your feet and stop yourself from flailing around in the water, or when your boss adds another 10% to your workload when you're already at capacity—*Argghhh!*

Whether you're new to the working world or someone who's a veritable veteran, it's common to feel overwhelmed, overtired, overworked, or like you're at the end of your rope. Yet how many of these emotions are problems that *you* have the power to solve? Navigating the workplace can be tricky, and if you don't know the rules, it can make the learning process a little rocky. But don't worry— you *can* manage all of this by using a few practical tips that you can employ along the way.

This short book is here to give actionable, real-world steps to both young people who are new to the workforce and to workplace veterans

Successful Habits for Work

who could use a new perspective to add to their wisdom. This guide will help you break into the workforce with a little more ease, confidence, and clarity as to what to expect in the workplace.

Chapter One

The Habit of Anticipating Needs

ANTICIPATING THE NEEDS OF OTHERS… hmmm, that probably sounds like a tough gig to tackle. However, if you master this skill, it'll make you an *invaluable* asset to both your colleagues and your superiors. Anticipating others' needs demonstrates your capability to remain agile, be a creative problem solver, and assist in the growth of your company.

According to the Forbes Coaches Council (2018), if you make *yourself* the reward, this will trigger positive emotions from your colleagues and make them want to work with you. How do you do this? Well, you could consider…

Stockpiling company resources, such as human resource links, training documents for your role, special forms that your team will most likely need, contracts, and regularly-used stationery. Having these on hand can make your life *and* your colleague's lives a whole lot easier. You might find your colleagues asking you, "Hey, do you remember that document from training yesterday? I can't find it anywhere!" Here you come, riding in on your trusty steed with the antidote to eliminate their stress. It's a good feeling, and soon enough, you may find that the old saying "*a gift opens the way for the giver*" rings true; soon enough, you may find your colleagues asking you how they can help you!

Volunteering on the coveted coffee run—*This is a huge one.* Coffee is the elixir of the gods during the day-to-day grind. "Who drinks the mocha latte, and who wants a flat white with two sugars?" A small gesture, right? This gesture shows you care and creates a feel-good atmosphere amongst your colleagues. This small token of goodwill can boost their day and reset the vibe in the office; cheers to you. You can get bonus brownie points if you remember the boss's coffee order. If the door is open to their office you can knock and let them know, and now you'll start to look like the leader of team morale that you truly are.

Knowing the good lunch spots. As much as you may love your work, many water cooler conversations involve where and *what* to eat at lunch. Colleagues will want to know where the good coffee is and what they should avoid! Imagine your coworkers saying "Ask Michael, he knows, he does the morning coffee run." You'll position yourself as the company beacon of respite; you could also seal this deal by being the provider of afternoon snacks to get yourself and your colleagues over the 3:00 pm hump.

Sending daily inspirational or funny memes to your team if you work in an office can help keep morale high or put you in your team's memory banks (As long as your company policies allow it). Don't discount these menial tasks; it's the little things that put you in the right light with your peers. And trust me, your boss is taking notes.

Ask questions and pay attention to your surroundings so you can anticipate the needs of your colleagues and your superiors. What are the common themes popping up in your environment, and how are they connected to what you can provide or anticipate for the future? For example, if you work in warehousing and the drivers are constantly calling you asking for updates about changes to the manifest, you can anticipate this and have any new details prepared to send to them via email or in-person next time, which saves them time.

Anticipating customer needs and relaying vital information to both your colleagues and your superiors. For example, let's say that you work in a retail sports store. You find that over the past week, customers have been asking about the benefits of the latest golf driver, what the best brand is, and what the features and benefits are. You can help the customer by providing them with a printed copy of the features and benefits to take away with them, and you can help your colleagues by keeping extra photocopies under the front counter and alerting them about the trending questions. Not only is this a win-win for the customer, but you'll also catch your colleagues' and your superiors' attention and look like the hero of the situation.

This means that when they're talking about you behind your back, your colleagues are more likely to be saying "Whitney is awesome to work with. I'm glad she's on my shift. I can rely on her," than they are to be saying "Whitney is lazy and I curse the day she was born."

… Okay, okay that was a bit overdramatic, but you get what I'm saying, right? You want to be on the good side of your colleagues. If you extend your hand first, then when you find yourself requiring assistance in the workplace, others won't hesitate to back you up; the reciprocal cycle of giving and receiving will continue.

Anticipating needs could be applied in many scenarios. As another example, let's say you work at a grocery store and your colleague, Robert, is working on cash register seven. If you know he struggles to remember discount codes, you could leave a printout at his cash register and let him know about it. Robert would feel acknowledged and relieved to have the answer on hand, which will help boost his self-esteem and assist in elevating team morale. The action also demonstrates you leading by example, and your colleagues would, hopefully, follow suit.

Picking up the slack. This one is a delicate balance of making yourself available when you can versus overloading yourself to appease colleagues. You want to be refreshed enough to be able to assist first before you offer a hand. If, however, you have finished your set of tasks and you see an opening to offer a hand, jump in! Lift the load a little—in the long run, they will be thankful and repay the favor when you have a heavy workload.

Going the extra mile for your colleagues by anticipating and meeting their needs shows your willingness and leads to *many* benefits for you and your team, including:

- Creating allies
- Displaying your initiative and leadership abilities
- Cultivating a healthy workplace culture
- Building company loyalty and trust
- Breaking down barriers with peers
- Increasing your company value
- Making you relatable and approachable and your colleagues more likely to help you, should you ever need a favor
- Making yourself the indispensable go-to person

By creating and maintaining this habit through the steps outlined above, you put yourself in the running for a—drum roll please—promotion! Read on for more ways to better your chances of being promoted.

Chapter Two

The Habit of Always Knowing the Answers

DO YOU HAVE THE ANSWERS? Are you the wise oracle of your team? If you don't have the information, do you know who does or where to find it? This goes hand in hand with the points in chapter one. It may take some time for you to gather enough knowledge to fulfill this role, but it *can* be done. According to John. R. Katzenbach and Douglas K. Smith (qtd. in Amal et. al 2015), there are four main elements to discipline in a team: common commitment, performance goals, complementary skills, and mutual accountability. If you can fill your necessary niche, you contribute significantly to the greater whole. Here are some ways to become the wise one on your team:

Always print off important emails that you'll need to refer to repeatedly. If you ever get an email that isn't easy to reference or isn't comprehensive, retype it to make sense and print it off, keeping it easily accessible in case you need to reference it. On these printed emails, be sure to highlight key company dates. For example, if you work in a purchasing department, when is the next invoicing run? Are there major company holidays that people should know about? And the question everyone wants to have answered: when is payday? It's also important to keep track of changing details, like upcoming changes to payroll that people might miss or staff changes that will affect your team. You can keep a spreadsheet to keep track of these changes, too. Implementing these small, additional habits will put you ahead of the pack and well on the way to becoming a key member of your team.

Sometimes you won't have the answer; that's okay. If you've gone through all of your resources and exhausted all of your options, you simply have to think about who will have the answer in the company. It could be Jill in the warehouse or Marco in the retail sector, and maybe they can help you out with the next step. This brings me to the next point...

Do you know the people in your company outside of your team? Start building a rapport with different departments and be sure to make note of their names, job titles, and roles. This way, if a peer ever asks you a question that you can't answer, you'll likely know someone who can.

Learn the value of research. If the water in the well has run dry and nobody in the company knows the answer (which is rare but happens from time to time), can you research alternatives and try to find answers for your colleagues? See if you can contribute proactively by seeking out the answers. Your colleagues will love you for it, and who knows? You might be the one to stumble upon a way to complete a task that saves the company money. Do you see where I'm going here? You're one step closer to the promotion.

Provide complete, quality answers. Try to provide comprehensive answers. This helps you *and* the person you're answering because you'll only have to answer the question one time and you can provide more than one option for them, which looks mighty impressive. If you have all of your information well-organized and easy to reference, you'll be able to provide this kind of answer expediently.

Can you close the gap? If your company is low on resources (like in a start-up company, for example), having the answers and showing your resourcefulness by finding answers puts you in the driver's seat of authority amongst the company peers and gives the higher-ups a taste of your leadership qualities.

Delivering the answers at the right time. Knowing the answers is half the battle in the workplace; knowing when to distribute them is just as important. Nobody is impressed with the company know-it-all. If someone is looking for information that you have, give them some space to seek out the information from you.

Knowing how to deliver the answer. This is just as important as knowing when. Seek to be informative and helpful to your colleagues; this helps develop trust and the ring of cooperation continues for when you need an answer.

Know how to deal with certain customers, peers, and superiors. For example, if you know that Todd the manager in the fleet department is grumpy before 9:00 am, it's best for everyone to call him *after* his morning coffee. Pass on this information to your colleagues. Human nature and knowing how to navigate certain human quirks will help you and your colleagues be more efficient and avoid some pain.

Know the right questions to ask. The key to knowing the right answers is to know what questions to ask. Ask yourself if your question is productive to your team and their progress. If it is, that's probably a good start. For example, let's say you're a personal trainer. You notice that a few of your female clients are struggling with a certain type of exercise, so you might want to consider *why* that is so you can make adjustments to modify or address it. Since some women have difficulties developing their core strength, this could lead to back issues that impact their ability to perform certain exercises. With this knowledge, you could suggest a circuit of abdominal exercises to build their core strength and correct the issue.

Next, you can ask yourself if this is something you'd want to know if you were in the customer's or supervisor's shoes. Knowing what time Misty takes her yoga class might not be the information to retain if you work in finance—I mean, unless you want to join her class, but that's for another part of this book. But I digress.

Network, network, network. Distribute and exchange your business cards with others who are in similar industries to yours. Make sure you retain these key contacts within and outside of your company. You can keep these business cards in a folder at work, so if your team or superiors ask, you have another feather in your cap to connect them with helpful people. LinkedIn is another application in which you can connect with industry professionals, should there ever be a need for you to contact them.

If you've been taking my advice thus far, then you, my friend, are an employer's dream right now. Keep going. If you're at company-wide events, luncheons, seminars, or even just popping up to visit another department, have friendly conversations with your peers. You'll be surprised by how much you learn; people love to talk about themselves and what they're doing. Word of mouth and face-to-face conversations are good ways to keep you at the forefront of your colleagues' minds for the future.

By always having either the answer or the knowledge and willingness to seek out the answer, you'll be able to achieve the following over time:

- Being an authority in your department
- Contributing greatly to your team
- Being hard or even impossible to replace
- Building your self-esteem and confidence in your ability to do your job
- Adding extra skills to your resume, which can lead to promotions or job upgrades as you become a more valuable asset
- Demonstrating your adaptability and creative thinking
- Increasing income and/or projects, depending on the type of job you do

Chapter Three

The Habit of Reading the Room

THE ART OF READING THE ROOM is not only a work skill but a life skill as well. This one may take more time to master, but once you do, it'll assist you greatly. If you're wondering what I mean by "reading the room", consider this: have you ever walked into a room and felt like there was a cloak of doom cast over it? Or, let's flip the script; have you walked into a room and felt like sunshine was beaming out of everyone? That's a good room to walk into, much better than the first. No matter what room, meeting, organization, or circumstance you find yourself in, reading the room by practicing active listening (Tiret 2015) and reading nonverbal cues will take you a *long* way. According to LA psychologist Albert Mehrabian (qtd. in "Mehrabian's communication study" 2021), around 93% of communication is nonverbal, meaning that only 7% is conveyed via voice. So how do you utilize this form of communication? Try some of these strategies to get you started…

What's your timing like? Consider what's going on around you before making a poorly-timed joke. For example, are people in your department cracking down to meet their deadlines by the end of the month? Is Carol so stressed that steam is coming out of her ears? Maybe hold off on that joke, or you may get a few cutting glares that'll make you want to sink into your chair. You can tell it next time—or, if it's a bad dad joke, then maybe keep it to yourself. Checking your timing doesn't only include jokes, however; are people quiet and focused? You may need to lower your voice while asking questions so you don't disturb your colleagues. It's very important to keep an eye and ear out and consider your timing before drawing attention to yourself; your colleagues may become irritated with you or think you're insensitive if you don't. Lesson learned.

Observe the room or group *before* you chime in. There are many details you can take in while doing this so you can make an educated choice about how to occupy space in the room. Note the verbal *and* nonverbal communication, as nonverbal cues often say more than anything else. Are you well received? Are you connecting with the right people? How are people acting? Are they slouched down in their chairs with scowls on their faces? Who is connected to who? Are people compacted together in cliques? Is a group of senior management standing together, or are they mingling with their employees? Whose faces are open and friendly? Gravitate to the open spaces and pick the highest possible options to connect yourself with.

Make necessary adjustments. If people are getting tired or annoyed because it's been a long day, their eyes may glaze over and they may slouch. How can you improve the mood? You can consider getting water for the group or lightening the tone of the conversation to switch their focus for a minute. What topics are prompting reactions in your colleagues? Check the hierarchy of the groups and try to remain neutral or balanced in your responses if it causes a frown to arise. Chances are, something external may be affecting the person and the topic might be adding to their annoyance.

Say less. Be considerate and allow others to direct the conversation. You'll learn more by listening to what others are saying rather than speaking most of the time. They may let slip some golden nuggets, or it may lead you to keep away from gossip mills that'll do nothing for your career. Listen for topics that you can meaningfully contribute to; are people discussing their personal lives, like their kids and their hobbies? Connecting and sharing your passions with them will allow you to relate to them. They may also let slip some interesting information about the company, as well; For example, if a company is merging with another company, your colleagues may be concerned with their job security. The things you learn in these conversations can be very beneficial in the future.

Know the energy of your colleagues. Chances are that if you're working in an office, you'll become well acquainted with your colleagues. (You should try to, anyways—you're spending more time with them than your loved ones, sometimes.) If you know that Tim is disgruntled with Sheila's recent promotion because he's been at the company longer, but you *also* know that Sheila is more hard-working than Tim, popular with her colleagues, even-tempered, and reliable, it can give you a better feeling for the situation and how to navigate it. Stay objective and work to lead by example in this case.

You'll also want to avoid discussing your salary details on the job, as it is potentially one of the fastest ways to ruin your rapport with your colleagues and supervisors when the conversation isn't handled properly. You may be earning a much higher salary than them due to negotiations and hard work, and discussing a wage gap without tact can give the impression of a superiority complex. If the conversation arises, try giving them tips for earning a higher wage—remember, one favor can lead to a favor from them in the future.

Reading the (Zoom) room can be more difficult and take a little longer. As many jobs now have colleagues and teammates connecting over the internet, you might *only* be seeing your colleagues on Zoom calls. While this might take a little more time to master, the same principles apply. How are people showing up on the Zoom calls? What do their facial expressions indicate? Are people focused, enthusiastic, happy, or are they ho-hum and hoping to get off the call? Can you interject with a mood lifter and drop in the chat with your good vibes to start the meeting off on a good foot? If you can contribute by participating and providing feedback, this is helpful to your manager or peer leading the discussion. See how you can contribute in a positive and meaningful way.

If you are working remotely without regular contact, asking more questions and following up more often with the client or customer can make it easier to read the situation. Once you know where you stand with the client or customer, you can then adapt your approach to get the best possible outcome for your client and yourself.

Employ empathy. Put yourself in your colleagues' shoes for a moment. Let's imagine that your coworker Ted has a presentation on the value of biodegradable keep cups. Nobody wants to listen to a boring presentation for the next hour, and they know it will leave them more deflated than when they entered. Should Ted power through the presentation and inflict the audience with death by PowerPoint? Or will he pause, see the room is disengaged, and mix it up with customer stories about the cups and how great they are? He could also try making his presentation interactive by having the participants use the cups; interactive presentations are much more engaging and memorable.

Reading the room is a skill that is often overlooked, but it might be the one that opens up the pathway to *your* career success. Mastering it will help you accomplish the following:

- Harmonizing your relationships with your colleagues and your superiors
- Helping you empathize with other people and their circumstances
- Demonstrating that you have leadership capabilities in bringing together diverse groups of people
- Increasing your confidence that you can change the dynamic of the room
- Piecing together a well-rounded view of what obstacles you may have to tackle

Chapter Four

The Habit of Being Tidy

HAVE YOU EVER WALKED PAST a colleague's desk that looked like a garbage dump? (Yes, *that* colleague.) If you were looking for help, would you go to them? They *might* have the answers, but the crumbs forming a line down their chest and littering their keyboard would be the ultimate professional turn-off. Having a clean, neat desk promotes the idea that you're organized and competent. Besides, studies in neuroscience have shown that too much clutter can make it hard for people to concentrate and focus (McMains and Kastner 2011)—you don't want that to happen to you, too.

Brush your hair and clean your teeth. You need to look the part for your position. If you're dressed sloppily, you can expect less-than-favorable reactions. Do you want the promotion? Then you need to do the basics, like dressing to impress, brushing your teeth, using mouthwash, and brushing your hair. Make sure that your clothes are ironed and that you look half decent. Make sure that the bottoms of your shoes aren't falling out and that you don't have holes in your socks. In all seriousness, people *do* pay attention to how you are dressed in the workplace; it's important. The way that you show up to work reflects the energy you're bringing into work and how serious you are about your career, meaning that taking simple steps towards maintaining your hygiene can take you one step closer to climbing the career ladder.

Staying (digitally) tidy is important, too. If you can keep your digital files in order, you'll be able to avoid the stress of digging through every folder on your laptop. Not only is this a stressful process for you, but when your peers ask you questions, getting their answers quickly makes you appear much more organized. This task of organizing your files might seem tedious, but it will save you a humongous headache in the long run.

A scattered desk creates a scattered mind. While some people can only achieve a tidy end result by going through a messy process that requires multiple ideas, concepts, and items to be visible in front of them (Vohs et al 2013), in an office or retail environment, your boss might not take too kindly to it. Can you find your stationery when you need it? Your pens, your paperclips? If your coworker Robert asks to borrow your stapler, do you have it on hand and properly filled with staples, or do you have to rifle wildly through your drawers, finally handing him a stapler with a flustered face only for him to find that there are no staples inside it? You don't want Robert to sneer, hand it back, and tell you not to worry about it; you want to be able to hand it over without a second thought, maintaining your composed and professional appearance. Keeping your desk clear will help to decrease your stress level and allow you to think clearly because you don't have to exert the extra mental energy to find what you're looking for.

Respect you and your coworkers' shared spaces. If you work in a large, open-plan office, chances are that you're sharing desk space with another colleague. If you keep a messy space, it's probably going to irritate them; this could become a breeding ground for festering resentment. And not only will it be irritating, but it will be inefficient; you and your colleague will both be slowed down significantly if you have to search high and low for documents.

On the flip side of this, if you utilize work trays, label your shared folders and documents, keep wipes on deck to clean the phone, and have an easily accessible container to hold pens, pencils, and markers, this will create the expectation that everything has its place, which goes a long way to creating a cohesive environment. When you or your coworker need to refer to a document, you'll be able to find it quickly and easily, and your colleagues will be able to easily nab a pen when they need one.

Less chance of accidents. If everything is in its place, there will be significantly fewer hazards in your workspace. If you tidy up any trip hazards, hanging cords, or other hazards, there's less chance of you or your peers falling over something preventable. For example, if you work in retail, failing to clear away boxes stacked in the middle of the walkway is another hazard that could hurt you, your colleagues, or even a customer, and *we don't want any lawsuits*! Keep the section you're responsible for clean and neat. For a more serious example, if you're in a job where you operate heavy machinery like a forklift, then you *definitely* want to contribute to keeping the warehouse clean and clear. A clean warehouse is a safe warehouse, and a safe warehouse can prevent not only accidents but deaths from occurring.

Keeps germs at bay and the little insect gremlins away. Was that a roach I saw running across the desk? No, that's *not* a good luck bug, you're thinking of ladybugs. Always keep your work surfaces clean and clutter-free so you can avoid any dust mites or other insects making your space their home. You also never know if staff members have allergies, and if dust is kicking up every time you type on your keyboard, chances are that it's time for your desk to be cleaned. You don't want them to walk past your desk and start sneezing due to your lack of workplace hygiene. If you accidentally have a coffee spill over your keyboard make sure you clean it up thoroughly. Nobody wants to put their hand on your desk and find it hard to lift. If not cleaned it can lead to mold settling in and possibly exacerbate staff member's respiratory conditions.

It can also prevent your desk from being the breeding ground for bacteria and colds that travel throughout the office. If you work in an office and it's tightly contained in one space… if one person comes to work and is sick, then chances are another person is going to get sick. You want to prevent this where possible by getting into the habit of a weekly wipe down at your desk, or a more frequent wipe down if you come into contact with more people.

For example, if you work in a grocery store, it's even more important to keep your section clean and sanitary. If you work at a register serving customers, give it a regular spray. This will make the customers feel reassured that the place they shop is clean, neat, and tidy, which will increase the chances of your customers returning. This will be a huge positive for you!

Do your share. If you have a communal kitchen, make sure you clean up your mess. Don't leave mugs or other dishes in the sink for the next person to clean up; they won't be cleaned by the dish fairy. Cleaning up after yourself is respectful to your work colleagues and will set an example for the next person to not leave a mess.

As a whole, by keeping your workplace tidy, you promote a healthy, safe, and productive workplace with the following benefits:

- Increased productivity and efficiency.
- Good impressions with colleagues and superiors, who now know you can handle responsibility and take your job seriously.
- Good impressions with clients who visit the office.
- Reduced stress levels, because you know where everything is kept and what goes where.

- A high expectation is set for others when you contribute to making your workplace safer.
- Elevated morale.

Chapter Five

The Habit of Befriending the Underlings

UNDERLINGS, AS THE TERM WOULD IMPLY, are those who are less experienced than you, earn a lower wage, or have a subservient role in your workplace. However, do *not* make the mistake of thinking they don't deserve your acknowledgment or respect. They are much more valuable to the workplace than you think. According to Kieran Perry, an independent business advisor from the UK, having a mentor ensures businesses and people are focused on the right strategies and tasks to thrive (2020).

Become a pseudo mentor. Even though they may be assigned to someone else, they may warm more to you because they know it's not your *job* to look out for them—you're doing it because you care. It's also possible that the assigned mentor will not be compatible with the mentee, creating an uncomfortable situation for both of them. This is where you can create a neutral party and lend an ear to the newbie without them feeling threatened. By being in this position, you're able to help a newbie navigate the workplace culture and value system of the company. It provides them with a safe space to ask questions about other departments and their career progression pathway within or outside the company.

If you've been a part of this company for a long time, the relationship will benefit you as well. You'll be aware of new information that the company is distributing to newcomers, such as new training processes or new technology that the company hasn't had a chance to update older employees on. It's also highly likely that if thirty new staff members are hired into your office, *someone* in that group of hires will go on to be influential in your organization. Staying connected with new hires also ensures that you have your finger on the pulse and can learn how to work most effectively with the new group. This will open you up to a new network of staff who may prove to be valuable in the future.

And, if we hearken back to the earlier concept of giving favors so you can receive them later, if your mentee goes on to work in another department or ends up in a position to assist you in some way, they will likely remember how helpful you were to them. There's great value in building rapport with newbies, especially if you've had a hand in seeing them flourish. And who knows? This could even lead to the mentee singing your praises and placing you in a higher light to your superiors for a pay rise or a promotion.

Cultivate relationships with the receptionists. You never know what information you can receive. Receptionists are taking calls for all departments of the company and filtering it through to the right people, so naturally, they know who to contact and for what. For example, let's say that you work at a leasing company and you're having a hard time getting in touch with Mary in accounts. Because you have been building a friendly relationship with the receptionist that works on the switchboard, you can ask him:

"Hey, have you heard from Mary? I've been trying to contact her for the last couple of days."

"Oh, Mary! She's been off-site for the last couple of days. She must've forgotten to put her out-of-office function on. Let me send a general email; she'll be back tomorrow."

See? These small tidbits of information help the wheels from falling off and make things run smoothly.

Forming a relationship with the caretaker or security guard also makes sense. They hold the keys to your occupational kingdom, and they're also the ones that are going to order the good chair for you. You wanna be nice to them so you don't find yourself on a rickety chair! The security guard may be the one to look out for you if you have to work late or let you in the building early, and they might have information about who's coming and going from the company, as well.

The IT department will hold many people that you'll want to be on the good side of. If your computer has decided to pack it in for the day, it's the IT department that can fix it for you. If you don't keep your cool, the consequences could be dire. They may be slow to fix your computer or return your calls a bit later than before if you became angry with them last time. Take heed, be patient, and build a conversation with them on the phone if they are fixing something for you. Chances are they will appreciate it because many IT departments are rather isolated from the rest of the company when they're not traveling between departments on repairs. IT may also be the supplier of new computers; you want to be top of the list for new technology, not the bottom heap.

Talk to the cleaner, too. After all, they're keeping your workplace clean, neat, and sanitary. You never know what a smile or a kind word can do for you in the future. That cleaner may not always be a cleaner;

you never know how you can benefit the people you meet or how they can benefit you.

There are many benefits to being a mentor and acknowledging those who are associated with your working ecosystem. So, as the saying goes, never look down on someone unless you're helping them up! Some of the benefits might be immediate, but more of them will be noticed in the long run:

- You improve your communication and interpersonal skills.
- You gain the chance of learning and cultivating new ideas that your mentee has acquired.
- You'll possibly get praise and advancement in the company should you make a solid impact on your mentee's life.
- You'll gain new perspectives and boost your self-esteem because you will be able to communicate with all walks of life.
- You'll improve your leadership skills, which can lead you to more career opportunities.
- You'll get self-satisfaction in knowing you assisted another on their path in life.

Chapter Six

The Habit of Self-Care

SELF-CARE IS A HOT TOPIC, and for good reasons. Your level of self-care is paramount; you will be surprised at how big of a part this can play in your daily working life. Getting into regular habits that promote your physical, mental and spiritual wellbeing will lead you to greater heights of success. According to the American Institute of Stress, 83% of Americans experience workplace stress, and US businesses suffer greatly from stress-related illnesses (Milenkovic 2019). You don't have to become a statistic, though; here's how.

Don't reach for your phone as soon as you wake up. Give your body time to get into a good rhythm in the morning. Wiggle your toes and stretch out your hands, adjusting to the light of the day. We've become so attached to our gadgets that we've forgotten we're humans first of all! Go outside and allow the light to hit you and breathe in some fresh oxygen for a couple of minutes. Okay, okay, okay—*now* you can check your phone if you must. Even better if you don't have to check it until you arrive at work.

Exercise. Seems like a no-brainer, but it's not, especially with Americans leaning upward of the 80% mark for nonactivity according to The Physical Activity Guidelines of America. Exercise is especially important if you work in a corporate office and you're seated for most of the day. There's no blood flow running through those legs of yours,

Successful Habits for Work

and your body staying cramped in an unusual position for close to eight hours isn't helpful either. You may see the little cakes at the morning tea break and say to yourself "One more won't hurt, it's not a big deal," only to find a few months later you've gained twenty pounds. Now you have to buy new clothes and feel sluggish, grumpy, irritable, and unable to concentrate as much.

If you exercise early in the morning, then it's done and out of the way. Better yet, if you also park your car a few streets away from your work, you can walk to work and that way your exercise becomes an easy-to-incorporate part of your lifestyle. If you have a pushbike and you can manage a ride to work, you're working out without thinking about it. You can start the day feeling refreshed and knowing that you've already accomplished something. This will help boost your self-esteem and start the day on a winning foot.

The added benefit is that exercising regulates your cortisol levels, which reduces stress and allows you to think more clearly, making you more productive and alert at work. This weekly or daily habit can have a profound impact on your working life and you might find that colleagues ask you for workout tips. If work is stressful and you work in a fast-paced environment such as a call center, then it's even more important that you keep up a workout routine.

Eating a well-balanced diet. Again, this one seems like a no-brainer but is not so easy to maintain. However, it can be done. Start with small habits, like making your lunch and incorporating one to two pieces of fruit in your lunch bag. Opt for a lighter meal at lunch that's not going to leave you sleepy and wanting to nod off while you're on the phone to the client. Try to incorporate vegetables into your daily life, perhaps by cooking a stir fry that includes a vegetable medley. This will be tasty *and* nutritious! That's a win-win. Packing in all the essential nutrients during a workday or any day can be tough, so if you can add a morning smoothie or a juice where you can gain maximum nutrients, then this is a good option to incorporate.

We all love to eat out and get drinks with our coworkers occasionally, but if your coworkers like to do this more often than most, be aware of how these outings might affect you. You might want to skip a few of those now and then. By eating well, you're not fueling your body with trash. Think of the body as a machine: it can only function with the fuel you supply it. According to the Department of Neurosurgery and Physiological Sciences (2008), taking good care of this area of life has a massive impact on your cognitive function. We need to fuel our brains so they function well!

Meditate. For some people, this is easier said than done. If you can find an activity that allows your brain to slow down and focus on the task at hand, this is close to a meditative state that works just the same. Prayer is also a good form of meditation and can be very spiritually healing for some. It brings many people great solace and is a deep form of gratitude and has all kinds of benefits. Others may like to paint or do something creative. Garden, make tea, or do any activity that takes you out of your mind and grounds you into your body. There are many different ways this may manifest for people. Some may take a walk near the ocean to clear their head, and that works for them. Some may like coloring books, and this brings them some peace. Some people may like more high-octane activities like running to clear the cobwebs out. Yoga is also known to be a good stress reliever. Playing sports with friends or even listening to your favorite calm songs can bring you to a meditative state. Before you know it, that looming 3:00 deadline from work has swept away like the waves from your mind.

Take social media breaks. Technology is firmly entrenched in our lives and it's here to stay. It has both positive and negative effects. Most people on average have quite a few apps on their phones. Think about all the information your brain is consuming as you scroll down the page. Heavy social media users have often reported poor mental health, increased anxiety, and depression. Limit your use if you can. It's hard to go to any public place now and find people who are looking up at you when you're outside because they're busy looking at their phones. You're not *connecting* with people like you think, you're *disconnecting*. How is social media helping your work productivity? If you're looking at Instagram for a few minutes here, a few minutes there, chances are that you're not focused on your work. You don't want your boss to come along and catch you on your phone; *that's not a good look*. To avoid the temptation and give your brain a much-needed break, you can delete Facebook from your phone along with Instagram so you can only check it out on your computer when you get home.

Be kind to yourself. If you've had a hard day at work and you feel as if you didn't achieve anything, remember to take a step back and note what you *did* achieve for the day. If you're new at a job and other people are moving ahead and learning more than you, don't take it to heart. You have your uniqueness and comparing yourself to other people just leads to depression and low self-worth. Take time out of your day to do something that brings you joy, whether that's meeting up with your friends, taking your dog for a walk, or going out to dinner to reset.

If you make a few mistakes and you're feeling like a failure, just remember that most things are repetition, if you repeat the action enough times you will get good at it. Remind yourself no matter how many times you make a mistake you are worthy and things will pan out all in good time.

Journal and reflect. This is a good way to keep track of your development, your emotional patterns, your triggers, and how far you've come as a person while also getting any negative thoughts out on paper and putting them somewhere constructive. Did you set a goal? Did you achieve it? Why? Why not? Are you happy with your job? Have you done all you can to put yourself in a position to gain a pay rise? If you write and reflect, this may provide a path to the answers you seek. After some time of writing in your journal as you progress in life, you will see that you've come a long way and you're doing better than you think you are.

Self-care is a top priority for not only succeeding in your career but succeeding in life as well. Here are some of the benefits of taking care of yourself:

- Clarity of mind, body, and spirit, allowing you to make the best possible choices.
- The energy to take care of others after having properly taken care of yourself.
- Increased energy and zest for life.
- Better work performance and output, which puts you in a winning position.
- Better energy that makes you enjoyable to be around, improving your relationships inside and outside of work.
- Increased confidence and self-esteem; it's the feel-good, look good principle.
- Better sleeping patterns and internal peace.

Chapter Seven

The Habit of Understanding Your Environment

AS SEASONS CHANGE, CLIENTS MAY OVERWHELM YOU with demands for products and services at peak times, while at other times, the crickets can be heard from the forest. What to do? If you know the peaks and troughs of the industry, you'll be better equipped to navigate the changes. According to motivation and inspiration guru Tony Robbins, reviewing the triggers of business can put you one step ahead with the fluctuating demands of your market.

Prepare for upcoming busy periods. As the Christmas period approaches, most businesses prepare themselves in a myriad of ways. If you work in the retail sector, the Christmas holiday season will undoubtedly be a busy time for you. Preparation, foresight, and changes in staffing (such as casual staff coming on board for the Christmas period) will be crucial to manage customer expectations. In your planning meetings, you can make suggestions and predictions to your manager about what to stock based on the type of stock that ran out last season and other statistics and prior numbers in the same season. Can you have extra paperwork ready for Christmas casual staff that are likely to be employed due to the busy period? Will you have to work longer hours during this time? You want to prepare yourself physically and mentally for the role.

If you work in a corporate office, can you organize Christmas cards for the clients to be sent out ahead of time? You can make a fun exercise with your colleagues, and then Santa's little helpers don't need to be overtaxed. If you have a bunch of reporting due at the end of the month and you know this is also a busy time for the company, don't leave it until the last minute. Work on it steadily, that way when the reporting is due, you're not cramming it in and potentially making mistakes. If it is going to be busy in either a retail environment or a corporate environment, do you have all the documents and files required to get the job done? If you don't, you can prepare them ahead of time, leading to more efficiency and productivity.

Prepare for downtime by learning new skills. If you know there's going to be a lull and you don't want your workday to drag along, you can ask your boss if you could do a department swap or if you could sit with another colleague who does a different job from you. This will not only kill the boredom from the day dragging along, but you'll also have a new appreciation for the job your co-worker does. You might also create a new ally, especially if they know you're interested in what they do, and you'll open up to learning new skills that you might want to expand on in the future.

During the downtime, this is also great for catching up on overdue emails, following up with customers, networking with suppliers or connected industries in your field, and coming up with ideas or solutions to issues that you didn't have time for previously.

Prepare for changes in the weather. Does the weather affect your job? Do you work outdoors? For example, if you're a personal trainer who trains your clients outdoors, if the forecast is expecting a downpour, you'll want to organize an undercover or indoor venue for your clients to train in. If you're a camp counselor and you're leading a group of summer kids through the camp, then map out new activities for them to complete inside.

Prepare for visitors coming through the office. If you work in a corporation and you know that the annual big wig meetings are held at your location, make sure that you dress neat, your desk is in order, and you're on your game. You never know what might happen. Perhaps they see you shining in all your glory and remember you later on, and perhaps they ask about you and mention your name to management; your possibilities are infinite. For example, if you work in retail fashion and you have your interstate account manager sailing through to check on your sales quota and discuss your targets, have your pitch prepared as to how and why you did or didn't meet your targets and provide a solution if you didn't meet them.

Prepare for sudden changes that may have been experienced in the past. If you work in a warehouse environment and all of the power stops working, what are the next steps to get the power back online? Are there documents explaining how to get the power back online, or does the backup generator kick in at a certain point? If you don't have documents for this type of incident and it happens regularly, what can you prepare for the future to make things run smoother?

Are you a truck or bus driver that has certain routes that are tricky to navigate? What can you do to save time on the route and be more efficient? If you prepare to look at the daily traffic reports and listen to the staff radio, you can keep up with the changes. Check in with your colleagues to see if anything has changed on the roads, and if they have, let your customers know that their delivery will be delayed rather than simply turning up late. The key is to be one step ahead so you can anticipate situations and not be caught off guard.

Successful Habits for Work

What type of place do you work in? Is your environment a fast-paced one where elements are constantly changing and there are lots of moving parts? If so, this means that your preparation and willingness to learn new skills and absorb information at a quick pace will be the name of the game. This will also tie into other habits to assist you on your path, such as getting enough sleep if you have to work at a high pace. Your ability to focus will be key. Do you work in a nursing home with a lot of elderly people? If this is the case, then your ability to display empathy and slow down your speech will be important. Patience will be the name of the game in this case.

In essence, knowing your environment and all that it encompasses will put you in the driver's seat and bring the following benefits:

- Less stress, because you are aware of what's coming next.
- Avoiding certain pitfalls that could have been prevented.
- A sense of confidence and pride, as you have everything under control.
- Demonstrates your capacity to become a leader in the organization.
- You look like the very competent person you are.

Chapter Eight

The Habit of a Good Night's Sleep

WAKING UP FROM A GOOD NIGHT'S SLEEP is one of the most refreshing ways to start the day. Sleep is an integral part of our day; one could even say it's the most important part. Sleep is where we rest our minds, our bodies, and our spirits. However, what's scary is that up to 34% of Americans get less than the recommended seven to nine hours of sleep per night (Center for Disease Control and Prevention 2017). So many of us are sleep-deprived, and this impacts not only our performance in day-to-day life but also our performance in the workplace in ways we wouldn't imagine. Here are some tips to help ensure a restful night.

Turn off your devices one hour before you hit the sheets. Do you have that iPhone near your bed? Well, its cheeky blue light is penetrating your eyes as you scroll through a few last funnies on Facebook before closing your eyes. *Put the phone down.* That LED blue light may be one of the elements compromising your sleep and causing eye strain. What actually happens is that blue light blocks the body's sleep chemicals, which is the very thing that helps you catch some zzzs. According to the Lighting Research Center, this habit can cause us to

Successful Habits for Work

wake up groggy the next day. That's not good for you or for anyone else in your life, be they at home or at work. Nobody wants to be on the receiving end of your irritation just because you couldn't put the phone down last night.

Tuck your phone away in your bedside drawer and place it on airplane mode. If you *must* do something to enter the wind-down phase for the night, turn on dim lights in your room to read by until you go to sleep. Don't worry, your phone will be there in the morning.

Get to sleep at the same time every night. This might sound a little boring, but it helps your body get into a rhythm so that your natural sleep cycle emerges. This will help you to feel more refreshed, and hopefully, you won't need as much caffeine as usual. It will increase your focus and clarity, you'll possess a brighter mood, you'll be ready to face the day, you'll have increased immune function, and if you drive to work, you'll be safer in your vehicle due to your alertness.

And don't hit that snooze button! Get up and allow the morning light to hit you. This also increases the probability of forming a great sleep pattern. Note that sleeping at the same time every night may be a different routine for different people depending on your job occupation and lifestyle. You might be a night shift worker that finishes at 6:00 am, so trying to be awake and alert when others are just starting their day is not going to work for you. Work to *your* schedule, remembering that the key is to sleep for seven to nine hours a night.

Prevention is the cure as sleep loss can seriously affect your work. If you are sleep-deprived, then it will take a lot more mental energy for you to focus on the task at hand. According to psychology professors from the University of Pennsylvania, this sleep deprivation may lead to more mistakes and mishaps (Lim and Dinges 2008). If you work in a high-pressure job where you have to be sharp and alert, this is going to prove to be a big issue in the long run. If you have an important phone call to take, you could miss it. If you work as an emergency nurse, delivering the wrong dosage to a patient could potentially be a deadly mistake. The fix is normally to reach for a coffee to top up your system to keep you functional, but excess coffee in the system can take up to eight hours to vacate the premises, thus making you super alert or jittery after work at a time when you should be settling in for the evening.

Sleep loss can also lead to weight gain because you're lacking energy. You're more likely to reach for the quick sugar hit rather than a piece of fruit or a healthy snack. This in turn leads to a cycle where your insulin levels spike for a short period and then crash. This potential weight gain in combination with a sedentary job can lead you down the road to type two diabetes, and that is *not* a road you want to travel. Quick, turn back!

Lack of sleep can lead to conflict with your colleagues and superiors. If you're grumpy from a lack of sleep, your colleagues are bound to notice. "Don't go near Dave this morning, he's roaring like an angry lion." A lack of sleep can make you irrational, angry, depressed, and hard to work with. You may overreact in a work situation that wouldn't be a big deal if you were fully alert and present, but without sleep, it might seem huge. At the far end of the scale, if you're constantly overtired and fatigued, this can lead to long-term consequences in and out of work. If you're difficult to deal with, word can get out, and this can lead to unnecessary headaches including your boss looking upon you unfavorably. If you're gunning for that promotion, it's definitely not going to help you along your way.

Assess your sleep routine. Do you have one? Do you read or journal before bed to get your mind to relax? Might be a tip to try. Are you out socializing with friends until late and this cuts into your sleeping time? Might be time to think about reining it in and letting your friends know you have to get some beauty rest. If they're good friends, they will understand. Is the room you sleep in restful? Make sure the surroundings in which you sleep are peaceful and harmonious. If you have clutter and a bunch of stuff stacked around your bedroom, this may make it hard for you to rest. Is the air clear, or do you have a dusty room that will keep you sneezing? These things make a difference when you're trying to get optimal rest. Make sleep a priority, especially when you have heavy workloads.

Get some help. If you have a more serious problem with your sleep patterns that you haven't been able to regulate, then it's time to seek help from your local doctor. They can help you make a plan so you can finally get some rest and quit walking around like a zombie.

There are so many benefits to getting quality sleep. By resting well, you can get an edge at work. It will leave you:

- Refreshed and rejuvenated, ready for the workday.
- Alert, with your cognitive function working at a high level.
- Empowered to manage your workload and get through the day productively.
- Able to power through the day without using stimulants.
- Pleasant to talk to for your peers and superiors.
- Healthier, as sleep improves your immune system.

Chapter Nine

The Habit of Understanding People's Habits

YOU KNOW THAT CLAUDE in the customer service department gets to his desk at about nine every morning, so he won't be free to answer calls until after ten because he's busy catching up on the previous day's emails. But how *do* you know this? You're aware because you've built a rapport with Claude, asking him when the best time is to get in contact with him, thus making Claude all the more appreciative and willing to assist you. Knowing the habits of your colleagues and your superiors can be the very habit that can lead you to success. Dr. Stephen Covey once weighed in on this matter in his book *The 7 Habits of Highly Effective People* with an oft-quoted piece of wisdom:

"If I were to summarize in one sentence the single most important principle I have learned in the field of interpersonal relations, it would be this: Seek first to understand, then to be understood."

Take note of this one and don't forget it; it's one of the most helpful mindsets to carry into your career.

Successful Habits for Work

Assess the urgency of your request. If you speak to someone in a department regularly, find out what their schedule looks like. If you work on a retail floor and your supervisor is working on a new catalog layout and tending to many tasks and staff, you can assess the urgency of your request before butting in. If it's not too serious or time-sensitive, it's probably best to find him in a quiet moment or even leave it for the team meeting.

However, if you work in the building department for a school and there's a burst water main, that's a little higher on the urgency scale; you could call your supervisor directly. You can also think about the request you have and try to figure out if it's something you can ask your peers or figure out and navigate yourself. Check the line of communication commands in your company so then you will know who to go to for the next steps if you have a request.

When to send that email. Yes, *that* email. Should I send a group email to my whole department about this issue, or can I wait and bring it up at the meeting? The first question: is it something the whole team could benefit from that you've identified as an issue? For example, if you establish a glitch with a product that could impact the reputation of the company, best to let them know as soon as you can. A well-timed email with that type of information will paint you in a good light and you could save the company from the loss of customers. The second question: who is the email for? Did you just email a request two hours ago with no response? If you email again you're clogging up that department's inbox and you're going to look like a pain. Once you send an email to a department, consider how busy they might be and be patient. If it's an urgent request, possibly because you work in an office with a customer waiting for a response, you can indicate this in the subject field. The third question: are you sending the email to the right department? By networking and understanding the inner workings of your company, you will know who to send it to and plan around their typical turnaround times.

What are the habits of your bosses? Are they mainly out of the office, but you know they spend the day in the office on Wednesdays? Or do you work in an open-plan office where you can easily access them at all times? Would your boss prefer you work with the team leaders first before going to them?

Learn the hierarchy of your organization so you know when and how to contact your superiors. Habits include the moods of your bosses. Before speaking, consider their demeanor. If your boss is a quick, dynamic individual you will have to speak succinctly and get straight to the point, whereas someone else may have a boss who is more willing to take the time out of their day to listen to what you have to say.

Once you know your superiors' habits, it will make your pathway to them clearer, and if done right, they will take note for the future. Is your boss more friendly and engaging with her team? If so, try to remember what she told you about the new couch she picked up on the weekend so you can mirror back to her. Do they like certain things or have certain hobbies? Bring them up; this shows you care and if you have a request down the line it may put you in good standing with them. If you listen to people, they will likely listen to you.

What drives your colleagues and superiors? This links into the ability to read the room. Are you aware that while Marcus is currently working in customer service, he's more interested in working in finance, so he leans towards finance-related tasks? If you work with Marcus in your department and you're buddied up with him on a project or your work closely, you can play to his strengths and allow him to work on the financial elements of tasks while you work on another area that you have more interest in. It's a win-win; you're assisting your colleague on his way to his progression and you get to work on tasks that you're suited to.

Do you know where you fit in the goals of the company and the scope of the puzzle? For example, if your company's goal is to make 10x the profits for the year, it will likely trickle down to your manager and your department would then be laser-focused on performance. You can contribute and work with those goalposts, doing your best to contribute to the overall picture. On the other hand, if the goals of the department or company are modest due to having a good prior quarter, it may be an opportunity to exceed expectations and set your personal bar a little higher.

Seek to understand before laying blame. Isao Yoshino is a lean expert who spent 40 years with Toyota, and in his time, gained serious wisdom about how to lead effectively. He is often quoted as saying: "Managers need to create a culture where people are not afraid of making mistakes. Everyone makes mistakes. We can learn many things from the mistakes we make" (qtd. in SCDigest Editorial Staff 2020). Try to imagine yourself in this scenario: you're working on a high-stakes project, and at some point, an action taken by your colleague doesn't go to plan. This can lead to frustration at times, especially if you have envisioned an outcome. But before you jump the gun, wait. What happened in the process? Is there a missing link? Is the mistake an opportunity for that link to be rejoined and a new process created wherein the mistake doesn't happen again? Always ask first; the answer may surprise you. At that point, a resolution can be sought out and a new process developed.

By seeking to understand the habits of your colleagues and your boss, you:

- Develop your communication style and learn from others' perspectives.
- Show that you're a team player.
- Create harmony and balance in the workplace.
- Demonstrate your compassion and well-roundedness as a team member.
- Show appreciation for their time and efforts.
- Demonstrate initiative and professionalism by understanding what's required of you.

Chapter Ten

The Habit of Taking Criticism Well

TAKING CRITICISM CAN BE A BITTER PILL for some people to swallow, whether young or old. This can be true for many reasons, especially if the criticism comes from colleagues or peers. Leon F. Seltzer, Ph.D., of Psychology Today posits that one reason we struggle taking criticism is because we place too much validation in what others think of us and link it with our identity (2009). If you are working for someone else or even in your own business, critique will come. Even the best people in the world have faced critiques to grow into who they became; it's part of the process of learning. If the person critiquing you has done it well, it'll feel more like a piece of advice or feedback that you can utilize to improve in your chosen field. In rare cases, it may not be well-meaning. Here's how to work with either sort.

Listen first. Wait for the person critiquing you to finish and really listen to what they're saying. Is there information you can glean from them? Is your colleague's feedback helpful to you?

For example, let's say you are working at the greengrocer's and the customer leaves without their receipt. A few customers later, that same customer returns to you asking for the receipt, and you have to scroll back through the receipts and print one for her. Your manager reminds you that you should ask every customer if they would like a receipt at the end of their order. That's constructive criticism, which can help you with your job. A good response is to say "Thank you for the feedback." It gives you time to process the information and make an informed choice of how to respond. Step back first if you feel triggered by the criticism, and give it some breathing room if the critique is via email.

Ask follow-up questions. This makes the process more interactive and more of a conversation rather than a critique. If you truly don't understand the information provided to you, ask for a few more in-depth reasons as to why what you've done isn't working. For example, if you're working in an office environment, you might forget to send a document over to a client. Your peer raps you over the knuckles for it, but you don't think it's a big deal and you believe that the service can be moved forward without it. If you dare to ask more questions about it, your colleague may explain that without the document, the service provided is not legally binding, which may leave the company vulnerable. That's *definitely* criticism worth learning about, and it's probably better to hear it from your peer than from your boss.

Thank them. Even if the person giving you the feedback is a little snarky and you were meant to take it as a dig, which does happen sometimes, thank them. Then you can sit back and keep an objective point of view to see if there are any takeaways from what they mentioned. What can you consider for the next task? Can you add the information to your skillset? In addition, if you thank them it will throw them off guard. Try to keep a positive frame of mind and know it's nothing to do with you specifically. (Also, if they're just trying to nit-pick, it'll throw them off guard and put you in good standing for your capability to work with difficult people.)

Criticism can make your product or service better. Let's say you're a writer and you're biting your fingernails to see if your book will be well received by the public. You've received a review! Take a look over the reviews to see if there's anything you can learn to improve for the next book. If you're a copywriter or a fiction writer, you might have the reviews point out that you have an issue with your commas and a few other syntax errors. This might allow you to pick up these editing errors and produce a cleaner copy or manuscript for the next assignment. It's the same as if your favorite take-out pizza joint is always delivering your food cold and you drop their star rating due to it. If they take the feedback objectively, the next time you receive your pizza it should be piping hot and ready to eat!

Accept the criticism. They've provided the feedback, let it be as it is if it's valid. Once it's provided, you can address it as it relates to your job and decide to make changes and work to keep a positive frame of mind about the situation. For example, perhaps you've had a rough couple of days with long hours and your desk isn't clean when Marcy comes by. She may say "Your desk is messy. You should probably clean that up before Bruce comes back, you know he hates mess over everyone's desks." You *could* get offended and tell her how hard you've been working and how tired you are, *or* you could nod and agree, saying "You're right, I'm a little messy today." Most likely you'll clean your desk, but you don't have to take that feedback personally. If you look at it right, your colleague is looking out for you before your boss comes in to see your desk and you get an even bigger rap over the knuckles. She's got your back!

Decode destructive forms of criticism. It's most difficult to deal with destructive, invalid criticism. If there is a situation where you are being criticized for certain things and you know them not to be true, simply state the facts in a calm, clear manner. For example, if Evan comes past as you're working and you've just come out of the bathroom, he may say something snotty; "I know it was you that left the paper towel on the sink in the bathroom. You did that the last time." If this isn't true now, nor was it true before, just stay calm. "No, Evan, that wasn't me. Perhaps it was someone else." Remain neutral, keep eye contact, and watch your nonverbal cues as you reply.

In a different situation, if there is partial validity to what someone is saying, it can be addressed differently. This time, Evan may say "You are *always* missing that attachment and it's irritating." Still respond in a neutral tone. "Yes, I have missed it a time or two, sorry about that, but I haven't missed attaching it on *this* occasion." This is a way to not take it personally and avoid the sting of the attack. Sometimes people are just projecting; developing your self-esteem will assist you to feel good about yourself no matter what another person has said to you. Remember that *you are good enough*, otherwise, you wouldn't have been given the job.

If you can handle this area of life with grace and self-respect, it will help you not only in your work life but also in your home life. Learning to take criticism well has the following benefits:

- You can get an edge on the competition or in your job.
- You're demonstrating that you can handle high-responsibility positions that require an adequate response to feedback.
- You can navigate life smoother, as your worth is not tied to how others view you.
- You may learn new things about areas of work that have become an oversight to you.
- You can become stronger as you navigate through your workplace and hone your skills.

Chapter Eleven

The Habit of Being Adaptable

IS YOUR COMPANY FAST-PACED with a variety of tasks to complete? If a high-priority task arises while you're in the middle of completing another one, can you switch and be adaptable to these changes? This is a skill rooted in another one of those big life takeaways: the only constant in life is change. It's important to reframe our mindsets regarding traditional workplaces, especially in modern environments (Keith et al 2021).

Becoming adaptable provides you with career opportunities. It's a good idea to master a skill or chosen area, but consider the possibilities within that realm once you have. If you're flexible and open to learning new skills, you have the opportunity to stretch yourself right into a new job and keep yourself fresh. If you are asked to perform a task in your work department that you've never done before, take a chance! You might find new talents or skills that you never knew you had.

You will be a more valuable and well-rounded employee. The more skills you have, the more valuable you are to a company, as you can perform a variety of roles and you can fit into different scenarios easily. Let's say that Ross works in a different department than you, but has volunteered for several shifts in your department due to being short on staff. Now, a part-time position has opened up, and his manager suggests it might be a good stepping stone for him. If Ross didn't take those shifts, he wouldn't have those skills, and therefore wouldn't have been able to step into that role. You never know what opportunities lie around the corner; bosses will take note and this can lead to more avenues for success in your chosen workplace.

You will be more confident in any workplace. If you have the willingness and capability to take on new skills in a workplace, this will allow you to be able to move with the ever-changing tide of the world. As we've seen with the impact of COVID-19, a pandemic or economic downturn (or both) can spell disaster for workers who are not adaptable. However, if you practice flexibility, you will be able to withstand the challenges. Many workers are now working remotely and adapting to working digitally, which opens up new possibilities that weren't sought after previously. Your confidence will soar if you have the courage to try new jobs and not limit yourself. The more nimble you are in learning, the smoother things will be in your working life. Being able to adapt will also make you more confident that you can contribute to your family unit in whatever capacity you see fit. If you're just starting out in the workplace, it can give you the confidence to know that, no matter what, you *will* find another job.

How are your current skills transferable to different roles? If you have been a retail manager before, consider how this may make you suitable to be a rostering and staff manager or an event manager. The overall base of the skill is your penchant for guiding large groups of people and understanding who works best in what role. If Rebecca works at the marina as a tour guide and enjoys showing tourists the beauty of the locale, this could transfer to many other roles. These could include being a travel vlogger, working as a bus tour guide, working at the tourist bureau, working in sales, and so on. Due to her ability to talk to a crowd and sell them the view, it might be a product in the future. Widen your lens and you will see a world of work ventures applicable to you.

Learning new things will keep you feeling fresh and fulfilled. If you're plodding along all the time and working in a less-than-robust job, the likelihood of becoming bored is very high. You might start to slip and become complacent, depressed, and worn out due to the lack of change in your role. For example, Penny has been working at her local gas station for the last four years without any changes to her role. She checks in and she checks out and collects her check like a robot. She's feeling despondent about it and doesn't know what to do. Sally, however, has been seeking out ways to diversify her time at the gas station by asking for new cash handling responsibilities and changing to the night shift so she can learn how to close the gas station. Which person do you think will be more excited about going to work? Even if your current job doesn't allow for movement, try out new courses or dive deeper into your role to see what you can learn. Having a certificate or further qualifications never hurts.

The road to leadership is being paved. As a manager, CEO, supervisor, or business owner, the workplace is never carved in stone. There are many changes that can cause a business to fluctuate. If you are able to think quickly on your feet, pivot at crucial times, and read the next plays in the organization, this will demonstrate that there's potential for you to become a strong leader. You will be focused, open-minded, and able to manage things as a whole.

Ask questions to learn. How did you perform that task? Can you show me how to do that? These are questions you can ask your peers in order to learn and grow. The answers will help you in your current job and beyond. If Tim works in sales at the local car yard, he might start to ask his boss what other tasks he performs and consider learning about those tasks with a growth mindset.

Successful Habits for Work

Be okay with making mistakes. If you are learning new things, it's inevitable you will make mistakes. If you do, don't beat yourself up. Continue to focus on how to improve rather than focusing on how to be perfect. Enjoy the journey itself. The great thing about making a mistake is that you're pushing yourself to discover how to complete new tasks and you'll be able to share your knowledge with those around you so they don't make the same mistakes.

Your ability to adapt will lead to the following benefits:

- More career opportunities being open to you.
- Confidence that you can manage unforeseen work changes in your life.
- Growth, both professionally and personally.
- Increased leadership abilities due to your flexibility.
- Increased value as an employee.
- Increased happiness and decreased stress, as you will have more options available to you.

Chapter Twelve

The Habit of Prioritizing

ALERT—DEADLINES ARE LOOMING! You're working and you have two projects in front of you. One is due in a month, and it's simpler than the other one. One is due in two weeks, but it's harder to complete. Which one do you tackle first? While you're working that one out, your boss asks you to cover lunch for Ellen and complete an urgent task, not to mention all the emails that are backed up in your inbox. A study from Loughborough University in the UK indicated that the overload of emails caused increased stress responses in workers (qtd. in Loughborough Echo 2013). Don't fret—help is on the way. Here are a few handy tips to help you sort out your time management.

Develop a system. If you work in an office and your job is admin-heavy, work out a color-coding system to categorize the emails coming in. For example, if your boss sends urgent tasks and you know that they need to be completed immediately, mark them with an eye-catching color to make sure it stands out. If you receive emails from the team, mark those in a different color so they're easy to pick out from your inbox. (And remember to read those, too! They may vary in importance.) If you receive emails from other departments, mark these in the rank of urgency also. This will help keep you calm and alert and give you a place to start when tackling your inbox.

Check your due dates and assess the complexity of the task. If you have a task due in five days and it's something you know how to do like the back of your hand, but you have another due in two weeks which takes more effort, tackle the easiest task first. This can help you build momentum towards the second task. Researchers Francesca Gino and Bradley Staats have concluded that completing easy-to-do tasks boosts your mood and releases dopamine, giving you the necessary good feelings to dive into your harder tasks (2016). Now that essay doesn't seem so hard, does it?

There's another school of thought which feels that if you address the tougher project first, it makes the other task seem like a piece of cake. This may be something you want to test for yourself to see how *you* function best, but if you know that you fade like a wilting flower in the afternoon, it may be better for you to work on the complex task in bite-sized chunks in the morning and then finish your day with easier tasks. Just be aware that if your boss has an urgent task that has to be completed, then that's the number one priority to get started on if you want to stay on their good side.

Learn to delegate. If you have a workload that's not feasible for you to complete on your own and your colleagues are looking around for things to do, you can delegate responsibilities to them. This will free up your time and allow you to stay on track for the tasks you need to complete.

Use a time-blocking method. If you have a habit of wandering down rabbit holes, use a time block method by working backward on your projects. For example, if you have a large article to write for a client and you establish that it will take you about five hours to complete, and you also have a shorter article and you have to research certain elements, block out time for both tasks with a timer so you stick to it. Allow for breaks on either side and be flexible. You will be surprised how these small methods can help you stay on track.

Write a list. Keep the list manageable and don't try to jam-pack it with tasks and responsibilities, otherwise, you may feel overwhelmed and disappointed that you didn't complete your list. There's nothing worse than looking at a list to see that it still has a bunch of items on it. It sure feels good to check them off, though, doesn't it? Keep it to a maximum of three to four major tasks for the day. If there are small micro-tasks within that and you know you can reach them, then go for it!

Use tools to assist you with time management. Let's say that Dave is a social media manager and he has to complete three videos for Youtube, Instagram, and Facebook. Instead of creating three different pieces of content, he can create one large piece of content and change the introductions for each platform. He can also schedule the posts for a certain point in the day by using a software tool that uploads to all three platforms simultaneously. That's working *smarter*, not harder.

If you work in an office and you often have pre-set information that you send to clients, you can keep a list of templated words and cut and paste them when you need to to keep things running smoothly and efficiently. If you have meetings back-to-back all week, you can set up alerts by putting the information in your calendar and linking it to your phone to remind you at your chosen time. Take a look at some time management tools online; they may save you quite a lot of time in the fast-paced work society that we currently live in.

Establish boundaries and manage expectations. This includes eliminating distractions. If your colleague comes over and asks you to drop what you're doing to help with their task, you may need to politely tell them that you have other tasks with higher priority, but you'll be able to work on theirs in the future. Provide a date and follow-up if you can't get to it right away. You can also employ this method if you're working with a client. Let them know if you're not currently capable of completing the task, when you *should* be able to, and if you're delayed, offer another deadline and stick to it.

With the rise of social media, it's easy to take a sneaky glance at your phone, but those ten minutes scrolling five times a day add up. Put your phone out of sight if you have to concentrate on a task; you'll pat yourself on the back later.

If you can prioritize your workload effectively, this can set you apart in leaps and bounds. Here are some important benefits:

- By managing your time, you can achieve more in your workday.
- You will reach your goals quicker.
- You will demonstrate your worth to your company.
- Your ability to consistently complete your tasks by using a system can and will lead to bonuses and promotions.
- You will be more confident and see further progression in your career.
- You will free up time for other activities in your life.
- You will have less stress!

Final Words

NOW THAT YOU HAVE PLENTY OF TIPS on healthy habits that benefit you both in the workplace and at home in your everyday life, it's time to implement these changes. Each of these tips are simple, yet incredibly powerful and effective. However, I also have some specific areas of focus that will help immensely.

Given the fast pace of our society and the rapid changes we are experiencing, the main areas to focus on would be your time management and ability to eliminate distractions. Maximize your time and learn to prioritize and stay focused. Self-care is of optimal importance in order to succeed in your professional life. This includes taking care of your mental health, working on things that bring you joy outside of work, and building self-worth before you step into the workplace. This is very important, as the workplace is the environment where the challenges of interpersonal relationships will take a front seat. Strive to take a holistic approach to your work, as your life works like a spiderweb; all areas are required in order to bring forth what you want to accomplish in life.

Overall, the workplace—no matter where you work or what type of job you do—is a place of learning and tremendous growth. Each person has their own special qualities, and every person can be a valuable puzzle piece and feel fulfilled in their day-to-day roles. This

Successful Habits for Work

includes *you*. Hopefully, these tips can give you a birds-eye view of what to expect, whether you're just entering the workforce or you're already knee-deep in it.

Best of luck out there, and remember—*you got this!*

About the Author

DARREN CODDEL HAS YEARS OF EXPERIENCE working in the retail and fitness industries, as well as emergency services. He has also worked with disadvantaged youth to help them develop crucial social and teamwork skills. During his time working with others, Darren developed a habit of watching how others behaved in various scenarios. Observing these behaviours aided Darren in further understanding the dynamics between people and why they react the way they do. Darren has a passion for assisting others in building confidence and pride in themselves. He's always ready to help solve a problem, and Darren considers these traits a large part of the reason he turned to writing self-help books. He viewed writing as an opportunity to share the knowledge he had collected over the years.

When Darren isn't working, he loves to cycle, swim, work out, go bowling with his family, and defend his status as the reigning king of table tennis. Darren enjoys writing in a variety of formats, including poetry. Darren Coddel lives in Essex, England, with his wife of 14 years, their two children, and a cat named London.

References

Chapter One:

Forbes Coaches Council. "15 Top Tips To Become A Better Team Player At Work." *Forbes*, last modified December 18, 2018, https://www.forbes.com/sites/forbescoachescouncil/2018/12/18/15-top-tips-to-become-a-better-team-player-at-work/?sh=6b57e0b93f6e.

Chapter Two:

Amal, Bushra, Bela Munir, Muniba Iqbal, Tooba Ashfaq, and Syed Waleed Ahmed. "Organizational Behavior: Report on Team Work." *Slideshare*, last modified May 26, 2015, https://www.slideshare.net/ujahangir/team-work-report.

Chapter Three:

"Mehrabian's communication study." *Changing Minds*, accessed July 8th 2021, http://changingminds.org/explanations/behaviors/body_language/mehrabian.htm.

Tiret, Holly. "The importance of listening skills." *Michigan State University Extension*, last modified November 23, 2015, https://www.canr.msu.edu/news/the_importance_of_listening_skills.

Chapter Four:

McMains, Stephanie and Sabine Kastner. "Interactions of top-down and bottom-up mechanisms in human visual cortex." *National Library of Medicine*, published January 12 2011, https://pubmed.ncbi.nlm.nih.gov/21228167/.

Vohs, Kathleen, Joseph Redden, and Ryan Rahinel. "Tidy Desk or Messy Desk? Each Has Its Benefits." *Association for Psychological Science*, published August 6 2013, https://www.psychologicalscience.org/news/releases/tidy-desk-or-messy-desk-each-has-its-benefits.html.

Chapter Five:

Strain, Carrol. "Do You Really Need a Mentor?" *Business Opportunities*, published January 27 2020, https://www.business-opportunities.biz/2020/01/27/do-you-need-mentor/.

Chapter Six:

Gómez-Pinilla, Fernando. "Brain foods: the effects of nutrients on brain function." *US National Library of Medicine*, published January 12 2010, ncbi.nlm.nih.gov/pmc/articles/PMC2805706/.

Milenkovic, Milja. "42 Worrying Workplace Stress Statistics." *The American Institute of Stress*, published September 25th 2019, https://www.stress.org/42-worrying-workplace-stress-statistics.

Piercy, Katrina L, Richard P. Troiano, and Rachel M. Ballard. "The Physical Activity Guideline for Americans." *JAMA Network*, published November 20, 2018, https://jamanetwork.com/journals/jama/article-abstract/2712935.

Chapter Seven

Robbins, Tony. "Anticipation is Power: Turning Potential Business Problems into Opportunities." *Tony Robbins*, accessed July 8th 2021, https://www.tonyrobbins.com/career-business/anticipation-is-power-turning-potential-business-problems-into-opportunities/.

Chapter Eight

Centers for Disease Control and Prevention. "Data and Statistics." Last updated May 2 2017, https://www.cdc.gov/sleep/data_statistics.html.

Lim, Julian and David F Dinges. "Sleep deprivation and vigilant attention." *National Library of Medicine*, published 2008, https://pubmed.ncbi.nlm.nih.gov/18591490/.

The Lighting Research Center. "Lighting for Healthy Living." Accessed July 8th 2021, https://www.lrc.rpi.edu/healthyliving/.

Chapter Ten

Seltzer, Leon F Ph.D. "Why Criticism Is So Hard To Take (Part 1)." *Psychology Today*, published January 30 2009, https://www.psychologytoday.com/gb/blog/evolution-the-self/200901/why-criticism-is-so-hard-take-part-1.

Chapter Eleven

Keith, Drew, John Guziak, Lisa Manzati, Giovanna Mantovani, Eliana Pagnutti, and Francesco Frigenti. "First comes the workforce: The human-centric future of work." *Deloitte*, published January 15 2021, https://www2.deloitte.com/us/en/insights/focus/technology-and-the-future-of-work/future-of-work-research-workplace-adaptability.html.

Chapter Twelve

Gino, Francesca and Bradley Staats. "Your Desire to Get Things Done Can Undermine Your Effectiveness." *Harvard Business Review*, published

March 22 2016, https://hbr.org/2016/03/your-desire-to-get-things-done-can-undermine-your-effectiveness.

Loughborough Echo. "Email – yet more stress at the office?" Last updated October 3, 2013, https://www.loughboroughecho.net/news/local-news/email--yet-more-stress-5806726.

Thank you for purchasing and reading this book. I hope that you enjoyed it and that it has added value to your life. If you enjoyed reading this book and found some benefit in it, I'd love your support and hope that you could take a moment to post a review on Amazon.

For information on future Darren Coddel releases, please sign up to the mailing list at:

https://mailchi.mp/e6209b262397/darren-coddel

Printed in Great Britain
by Amazon